AF496622

A VIEW OF AVALON

Glastonbury, Wells and
The Somerset Levels

A VIEW OF AVALON

Glastonbury, Wells and
The Somerset Levels

Also Merlin let make by his subtilty that Balin's sword was put in a marble stone standing upright as great as a mill stone, and the stone hoved always above the water and did many years, and so by adventure it swam down the stream to the City of Camelot,...
THOMAS MALORY   c1400

An evocative view of Somerset by BOB CROXFORD

Published by ATMOSPHERE

A VIEW OF AVALON

*First published by ATMOSPHERE in 2001
Willis Vean
Mullion
Helston Cornwall TR12 7DF
TEL: 01326 240 180
FAX: 01326 240 900
www.atmosphere.co.uk*

ISBN 09521850 6 7

*Designed by Ann Butcher
Scanning by Formatrix, Exeter
Printed and bound by L.E.G.O. in Italy*

Also by BOB CROXFORD

FROM CORNWALL WITH LOVE	*ISBN 09521850 0 8*
FROM DEVON WITH LOVE	*ISBN 09521850 1 6*
FROM BATH WITH LOVE	*ISBN 09521850 2 4*
FROM DORSET WITH LOVE	*ISBN 09521850 3 2*
FROM THE COTSWOLDS WITH LOVE	*ISBN 09521850 4 0*
HAMPSHIRE	*ISBN 09521850 5 9*
THE CORNISH COAST	*ISBN 09521850 7 5*

COVER PICTURE: Burrowbridge Mump
FRONTISPIECE: Taunton Castle

CONTENTS

Imagine standing on the edge of the MENDIP HILLS a few ten thousand years ago. The view to the south would have been a shallow sea stretching into the far distance. Here and there a hillock or a hill, a bump or a mump would rise above a watery land. Eventually the sea receded; partly by natural means and partly by man's endeavours. By the simple process of allowing river waters to drain away at low tide and closing sea gates to stop water flooding back when the tide was high, the sea and salt marshes became land. The sea view disappeared and the Mendip ridge offered a view of the MYSTICAL LAND OF AVALON. Occasionally this view would revert to a scene from earlier times when the sea defences were breached by stormy weather and gales in the Severn Estuary near BURNHAM-ON-SEA. Flood waters would sweep inland taking men and women, cattle and sheep, buildings and barns before it. In 1607 and other years in the 17thC GLASTONBURY became an island once more as tumultuous sea waters raced across twenty miles of land. Now the problems are winter rains which can lie on the flat earth for months. But in spring and summer when wild flowers line the roads, the sound of birdsong is in the air and the water in the drains is low and still the land becomes magical.

THE MENDIP HILLS are a mysterious place. Where the VALE OF AVALON has small hills, the MENDIP plateau has small depressions.

The geology is different. Limestone caverns and underground rivers have drained the land. Gorges and subsidence show signs of this erosion. Some of the holes are man made and stretch back to lead mining before the arrival of the Romans to these shores. Descending from the plateau the moors of Avalon are a flat and at first glance a boring landscape of level fields, drainage ditches, peat bogs, willow trees and the occasional hill. The area is effectively divided by the POLDEN HILLS. These are only hills in the sense that they relieve the flatness of the surrounding land. Anywhere else and this low ridge would be regarded as a very minor geographic feature. Here on the SOMERSET LEVELS the importance of the POLDEN HILLS should not be underestimated. A road along the top had been an important artery long before the Romans built a road here. When GLASTONBURY became a centre for early christian worship communications across the land were essential. The GLASTONBURY ABBOTS maintained huge estates and built up a substantial power base across the country. Many of the local roads were originally connected to the Abbey.

In such a flat landscape the occurrence of a small hill became a matter of some interest. Anything which gives a sense of direction is to be welcomed. They are called hills, mumps, knolls, tors and ridges. It is around these hills that we navigate and gain a sense of distance. On the flat land the vanishing lines of drains and ditches give an even greater feeling of space.

The maintenance and repair of the sea defences and drains along the coast was the responsibility of everyone who lived under the threat of a breach. After one flood the Abbot organised over 500 men, women and children to repair the sea wall. Rich and poor alike joined in the heavy manual work because their lives and livelihood depended on it.

The Levels contain a varied selection of moors and low hills. Over forty square miles are either at, or slightly below, sea level. The task of keeping the sea out and the land dry has been going on for hundreds of years. Unfortunately one of the results of centuries of drainage has been the lowering of the surface level making the task during flood times even worse. In the 19thC steam engines were used to help drain the land.

Under the patronage of the church small towns flourished and grew rich on the wool trade. The area became famous for many different types of produce, from cheese to cider and from woollen goods to reed thatch. Unique methods of growth, harvest and production developed for almost all the local trades. Cheddar Cheese was made by several farmers pooling their milk into large cheeses. The harvesting of Withies was bid for by the men who would arrange the stripping of the shoots.

Goods were shipped to Bristol and other ports from wharves deep inland. Boats came up the River Parret as far as Langport. In medieval times goods were shipped to and from Glastonbury by boat.

The Mendip Hills are a plateau of pervious limestone. Over thousands of years rain water has cut into the soft rock until many of the streams have disappeared underground. Very occasionally there is sufficient waterproof material for small ponds and lakes to form. The porosity of the land means that many of these are helped by the hand of man. The Priddy Nature Reserve has two small lakes which are a haven for water birds.
The area is distinguished by neat well-drained fields hedged with the local grey stone.

Cheddar Gorge is a famous example of the erosion of the Mendip edge where the river first cut a meandering zig-zag through the edge of the escarpment. Finding more soft rock below, the river eventually went underground where it continues to cut a course deep under the surface. This action has caused a number of caves to develop which are open to the public. The caves had a practical application in the making of Cheddar Cheese. The even temperature of the caves has proved perfect for the production of England's most ubiquitous cheese. Traditionally the milk was combined from several small dairy herds to make each large cheese. The farmers who pooled their milk in this way would be paid according to the amount of milk they contributed. In the period just before rail transport brought the rapid shipping of fresh produce the long lasting CHEDDAR CHEESE was highly valued. In early days the cheese was made slightly softer than it is today but the value of a cheese which could last for long sea voyages meant that the hard cheese we know now became the norm. Both WELLS and GLASTONBURY have a naturally spiritual ambiance. Even before Christianity arrived the existence of mineral springs with possible curative properties had a special significance.

The Romans were in WELLS in the early part of the first millennium but did not establish any major or lasting settlements in the area. In AD 705 a small church was built at a place of many natural springs. According to some geologists the water which goes underground in the Mendips surfaces years later in many parts of the lowlands. WELLS has a bountiful supply. King Ine built the first church at St. Adhelm's prompting.

At the beginning of the 10thC SOMERSET had grown in importance to establish its own diocese. Athelm was the first bishop. Giso of Lorraine was introduced to England by Edward the Confessor and was responsible for bringing the continental style of communal living for the monks. Giso's establishment was not to last as his successors moved the base to Bath. A Bishopric was re-established in WELLS about fifty years later. Almost 300 years were to pass before the building, which grew into the one we know today, was dedicated.

As a piece of gothic grandeur WELLS CATHEDRAL has few equals. Its bold structural design is awe inspiring; looking austere now without the original medieval coloured decoration. The mirrored Early English arches belie their nearly 800 year age. The recently restored west facade once contained over 300 carved figures.

The Chapter House is an elegant building where the English Gothic style reached its height.

Many visitors are amused by the animated clock. Mechanical figures appear each hour and perform a small tournament.

VICAR'S CLOSE to the north of the Cathedral is reputedly the oldest unchanged street of dwellings in the world.

The appreciation of time and historic events is never far away in this land. Some of the history is all too real while legends and fantasy blur the line between fact and fiction.

How old does a legend have to be before it is considered genuine?

In GLASTONBURY a lot older than elsewhere apparently. If a story first appears in the 11thC or 12thC it is considered disgracefully modern. Research seems a hopeless task. The Arthurian excavators, Christian writers, Roman scholars, *et al* seem to delight in claiming each tiny clue for themselves. Did CHRIST visit GLASTONBURY with his tin trading uncle JOSEPH OF ARIMETHEA? Did JOSEPH return and plant his staff which became the thorn tree on WEARYALL HILL? Was KING ARTHUR buried at GLASTONBURY ABBEY in the 5thC? Did KING ARTHUR stand on the A39 and cast EXCALIBER, his sword, into the RIVER BRUE? If so he must have made a habit of getting his sword wet because there are pools from Cornwall to Belgium which claim the same honour.

Professional storytellers in the days of the Abbey's fame were never short of new material. One thing is certain. Wherever these stories originated, whether in fact or fiction, GLASTONBURY is one of the best places to set them.

GLASTONBURY in modern times has become a centre for New Age spiritual ideas. Approaching the town from STREET there is a distinct shift of emphasis and ambiance. The shoe factory town of STREET is pleasant enough with massive modern sculptures on the by-pass, but as you enter GLASTONBURY the spiritual symbols are more tangible. High on the right is a special tree. This is WEARYALL HILL and the small thorn tree near its summit is reputed to have grown from the staff of JOSEPH OF ARIMITHEA. Legend recounts that he was "weary'all" and leant on his stick which took root.

What is certain is that GLASTONBURY was a very early place of christian worship in England. Although there is no direct evidence of pre-christian sacred use of the Tor, megalithic man saw deep significance in geographic features. The sculpted terraces on the side go way beyond the scale of strip lychetts. It was traditional for the early church to take over earlier sacred sites. Many times this was done in the name of St Michael. St Michael's church on Brent Tor in Devon, St Michael's Mount in Cornwall and Mont St Michel in France are all examples of this practice. Naturally the ruined church on the top of the Tor is dedicated to ST MICHAEL.

I was once told that London has only six places worth visiting for a visitor. GLASTONBURY has at least five; THE ABBEY, THE TOR, THE COUNTRY LIFE MUSEUM, THE TRIBUNIAL, a host of interest nearby and THE CHALICE WELL. The Well is a tangible demonstration of the way that the waters of the MENDIPS travel deep underground before providing a gushing spring miles away. At one time the land near the well was lower but thousands of years of sediment have buried it under the surface.

Beyond CHEDDAR under the lee of the MENDIP ridge lies AXBRIDGE. This village has many stylish old houses. Pride of place goes to a half timbered building in the corner of the main square. It is called

King John's Hunting Lodge but was built a hundred years after his death.

Wedmore is a charming village built on slightly higher ground than the moors which stretch into the distance on all sides. Before the time of draining the Levels, Wedmore would have often been an island.

Taunton Castle was once a great fortress. A small part is now in the grounds of the Castle Hotel. The Somerset County Museum now resides in part of the 13thC structure. It was here that Judge Jeffries held part of his *Bloody Assize* after the Monmouth Rebellion. The church of St. Mary's has a tower made more dramatic by the perspective of 18thC houses in Hammett Street. The town's most pleasant association, for many, is cider making.

The River Parrett was until recently an important navigable river as far as Langport. Bridgwater became a major trans-shipment point for goods from all over Somerset. As the last place where a bridge was practical before the sea it also became an important river crossing. Before the building of the newer bridges on the A38 and M5 the bridge at Bridgwater was a notorious bottleneck on the road to Devon and Cornwall. Pre-war motorists would talk at length of the time spent waiting to cross the bridge. The first traffic jams in the country reputedly started here.

The M5 motorway has now divorced the extreme western edge of the Somerset Levels from the rest of the area. The stretch of coast north and south of Burnham-on-Sea has sea defences which are vital to the drainage of the levels. The Abbots of Glastonbury controlled the maintenance of these works for hundreds of years through history. Without the protection of the dunes, dykes and associated sluices flood waters would sweep inland.

Langport was a port when the Domesday book mentioned it in 1086. The Romans built a causeway here when they realised the importance of the River Parret as a navigable access to the sea. It has been suggested that the houses in Bow Street have their fronts built on the substantial Roman Causeway which is why they lean backwards slightly into the softer foundations at the rear. The quiet town of Somerton is typical of Somerset. Stone buildings, a market cross and down to earth shops make it the epitome of what we expect of the area.

Although reed thatch is grown on the Levels there are few thatched cottages on the flat moors themselves. It is south of the Langport/Somerton ridge that thatch comes into its own. Magnificent examples can be seen in Isle Abbotts, Isle Brewers and Tuckington which give a whole new meaning to the word *picturesque.*

Large and small orchards flourish all over Somerset. Cider making is both a farm scale enterprise and major industry in the area. The perfect drink to wash down a chunk of Cheddar Cheese sitting under the shade of the ripening apples.

Stembridge Tower Mill at High Ham is the only remaining thatched windmill in England. It was built in 1822 and worked for nearly one hundred years.

Once there was a lake at MERE which has since been drained. In medieval times it was an important source of fresh fish for the Abbots and monks of GLASTONBURY ABBEY, especially at Lent. In the 14thC a fish house was built for the salting, drying and storing of fish.

The church tower at WESTONZOYLAND can be seen from miles across the flat Sedgemoor plain.   So too can the BURROWBRIDGE MUMP with its chapel perched on the top. With the chapel on the top of GLASTONBURY TOR one can imagine that church going in the past was as much as a keep fit exercise as an act of worship.

No history survives from the pre-historic castle on BRENT KNOLL. Legend associates King Arthur with the fort but some of the earthen structure date from even further back in time.

In many places the flatness of the Levels would create a boring landscape but here in Somerset the hills sometimes create a higher view point. The view from WALTON HILL when the weather is dramatic can be very exciting.

The history of the SOMERSET LEVELS are inextricably linked to the MONMOUTH REBELLION. The Duke of Monmouth's army was so ill equipped that it is also known as the Pitchfork Rebellion. Armed with little more than pitchforks the yeomen and farmers of Dorset, Devon and Somerset supported the Duke's ill conceived attempt to gain the throne of England.

King Charles II restored the monarchy to England after Oliver Cromwell's Republican Parliament. He allowed his success and the power of his Catholic influence to go to his head. He was not the type of man that many on the Royalist side had expected. Passions had become roused because the country had become used to the idea of the Protestant religion and did not see the virtue of a dissolute Catholic King. Some in the country saw the illegitimate Monmouth as a likely successor. Monmouth's supporters may have been clutching at straws when they decided that he had a reason-able claim to the throne.

The Duke arrived at Lyme Regis in 1665. There was no opposition because the town's mayor had used all the available gunpowder firing a salute to the King's birthday a few days before. Marching north at a slow pace the Duke gathered many of the local farmers and peasants to join his rag-tag army. In Taunton this motley band received a grand welcome. The good burghers of the town had a long history of independence and fighting for what they believed in.   Instead of showing decisiveness Monmouth vacillated and delayed. While the Royalist troops were still travelling across England at a slow pace he did not take advantage of the lack of opposition. He advanced on Bristol and changed his mind.

For a brief while he went to Wells. If Monmouth and his army are criticised it is because of his men's behaviour in and on Wells Cathedral. Short of bullets his men went onto the cathedral to strip lead from the roof. At the same time several acts of vandalism occurred. Statues on the facade were disfigured, damage which has only just been repaired 300 years later. Horses were stabled in the nave. Although this seems like a barbaric act of hooliganism it should be seen in the perspective of the situation at the time. Wells Cathedral was an exceptionally rich bishopric. As a landlord it owned farms and taxation rights over a wide area. In addition to farm rents, the tenants also had to pay tithes. Because Wells had always had strong links to Rome the Protestants saw the Cathedral at Wells as much a part of enemy territory as the King's Palace in London.

Although the King's men were still miles away the Duke returned to Bridgwater while he considered what to do. Still undecided, the situation was taken out of his hands by the arrival of the King's troops. Despite his time in the area Monmouth had not surveyed the territory or deigned to listen to local opinion. Using a telescope from the church tower he finally made a decision to engage in battle. Fatefully his forshortened view did not show a deep drainage ditch which became his downfall.

So sure were they of the rightness of their cause that his men went bravely into battle. Untrained and without proper arms his troops withstood the King's trained soldiers beyond all expectation. Many died on the battlefield without giving ground. Trapped by the drainage ditch they could not continue their charge through the opposing forces while the King's troops were able to access their flank with ease. Almost none of the survivors escaped capture as prisoners. That was the last military battle to be fought on English soil. Wounded and dispirited hundreds of the prisoners

were taken to nearby Westonzoyland Church. The conditions were terrible but worse was to come.

The infamous Judge Jeffries was appointed to try the rebels. He went to the task with sadistic relish sending men to the gallows twenty or thirty at a time. Some were tortured before their final execution. The Duke of Monmouth was caught fleeing the country and was sent to London for his execution reflecting perhaps on whether his indecisive character would really have made him fit to rule the country.

Charles II did not have long to reflect on his victory. In 1688 William of Orange, another Dutchman, landed in Devon. Marching straight on London he was victorious where Monmouth failed.

This book contains an anthology of writing on the area. There is much picturesque detail to be found in the journals of CELIA FIENNES and JOHN LELAND. Later writers include ARTHUR CONAN DOYLE's thrilling historical saga Micah Clarke set during the Monmouth Rebellion. For historical and factual detail GEOFFREY ASHE and DESMOND HAWKINS provide interesting reading.

I don't intend the preceding words to be in any way a guide, nor are the pictures in this book. The photographs are intended to give a feel and remembrance of this most interesting area of ENGLAND.

Bob Croxford August 2001

_T__here were two pools at Priddy, the Mineries and Waldegrave. It was
the Mineries that we locals called Priddy Pool, and in summer
children scrambled on its banks all day. At weekends middle-class
families picnicked on the tufted moorlands and parked their Volvos in
the layby. So how could a corpse as large as Larry's - how could any
corpse - stink and rot and float there undetected for thirty-six days
and nights?_

JOHN LE CARRÉ   1995   (from Our Game)

◀ _Priddy village green_
Mendip landscape ▶

*I*t was a blithesome morning. The sun was rising over the
distant hills, and heaven and earth were ruddy and golden.
*The trees in the wayside orchards were full of swarms of birds,
who chattered and sang until the air was full of their piping.
There was lightsomeness and gladness in every breath. The
wistful-eyed red Somerset kine stood along by the hedgerows,
casting great shadows down the fields and gazing at me as I
passed. Farm horses leaned over wooden gates, and snorted a
word of greeting to their glossy-coated brother. A great herd of
snowy-fleeced sheep streamed towards us over the hillside and
frisked and gambolled in the sunshine. All was innocent life,
from the lark which sang on high to the little shrew-mouse
which ran amongst the ripening corn, or the martin which
dashed away at the sound of my approach. All alive and all
innocent. What are we to think, my dear children, when we see
the beasts of the field full of kindness and virtue and gratitude?
Where is the superiority of which we talk?*

SIR ARTHUR CONAN DOYLE   1887

From Micah Clarke

Cheddar Gorge

*I*n the low Country, on the other Side Mendip Hills, lies Chedder, a Village pleaſantly ſituated under the very Ridge of a Piece of Ground, in which the whole Herd of the Cows, belonging to the Town, do feed; the Ground is exceeding rich, and as the whole Village are Cowkeepers, they take care to keep up the Goodneſs of the Soil, by agreeing to lay on large Quantities of Dung for manuring, and inriching the Land.

DANIEL DEFOE   1688

I lived 10 months in Somerset near Glastonbury and felt more at home there than I ever have anywhere. There was something there that I understood and that tolerated me. I loved that place and when my boys are out of what we call education I may well go back there to finish up. When, sitting here in New York, I think of Somerset, my stomach turns over with a curious kind of longing. It's beautiful country, of course, but there's something else that draws me.

JOHN STEINBECK   1952

◀ *Mendip Wall*

View of Vale of Avalon ▶

Perhaps we may consider it as a two-fold beauty, and firstly there is one beauty of aspect from a distance: who that has approached the city from over the top of Mendip, by bleak hill roads, over desolate rabbit-beaten tracts of stunted grass and moss, heather, or half burnt furze scrub, clambering the loose grey walls, traversing the forlorn ruins of the old Mineries, with their great settling lakes now grass with reeds and rushes, their mysterious half underground passages leading to fantastic chimney shafts, and then at last coming to the crest of the hill overlooking the old Bristol road - who that has done this and then for the first time sees Wells from that vantage point can ever forget the emotion it must arouse?

ROGER CLARK   1921

The West Front, Wells Cathedral

*T*here are many things which occur in the progreſs of a tour, and which one ought to ſee, not ſo much for the pleaſure the view of them affords, as for the fame of ſaying one has ſeen them. Of this number, I think, is the Cathedral of Wells; which, with all its antiquity, would not induce me to viſit that city, if it did not lay in the road to Bath. And yet ſhould any one obſerve, in a large company, that he had been at Wells, and did not viſit the Cathedral, four out of five would exclaim, "Not ſee the Cathedral? Oh Goth! oh Vandal!" ſo prevalent is the deſire of boaſting that one has ſeen every thing. But however to prove that, in this inſtance, I was neither a Goth nor a Vandal, it is neceſſary I ſhould give ſome account of what I really did ſee.

EDWARD DANIEL CLARKE   1791

Penniless Porch, Wells
Market Square, Wells

Croft Sheepskin
CROWN HOTEL

*I*t is related in annals of good credit that Lucius, king of the Britons, sent to Pope Eleutherius, thirteenth in succession from St Peter, to entreat, that he would dispel the darkness of Britain by the splendour of Christian instruction. This surely was the commendable deed of a magnanimous prince, eagerly to seek that faith, the mention of which had barely reached him, at a time when it was an object of persecution to almost every king and people to whom it was offered. In consequence, preachers, sent by Eleutherius, came into Britain, the effects of whose labours will remain for ever, although the rust of antiquity may have obliterated their names. By these was built the ancient church of St. Mary of Glastonbury, as faithful tradition has handed down through decaying time. Moreover there are documents of no small credit, which have been discovered in certain places to the following effect: "No other hands than those of the disciples of Christ erected the church of Glastonbury." Nor is it dissonant from probability : for if Philip, the Apostle, preached to the Gauls, as Freculphus relates in the fourth chapter of his second book, it may be believed that he also planted the word on this side of the channel also.

WILLIAM OF MALMESBURY   1095-1142

*Because whatsoever a man soweth, that shall he also reap,
I, in the act of laying the foundation of the church of
Glastonbury (which, being in my hands, has been reduced to
ashes by fire), do decree, by the persuasion of Heraclius, the
patriarch of Jerusalem, Baldwin, archbisop of Canterbury, and
many others, that, God willing, it shall be magnificently
completed by myself or by my heirs.*

KING HENRY II

*I knowe that England doe keep the right day that Christ was
borne on, above all the Nations of Christendome, because we
have a miracle hath often been seene in England upon that day, for
we have a tree in England, called the Holy Thorne, by Glassenbury
Abbey, nigh the Bathe, which on the 25 day of December, which is
our Christmasse day, hath constantly blossomed; which the people of
that place have received from antiquitie, that it was that kind of
thorne, wherewith Christ was crowned.*

JOHN EACHARD   1645

◀ *Glastonbury Dawn*

*W*hen Arthur bowed his haughty crest,
  No princess, veiled in azure vest,
Snatched him by Merlin's potent spell,
In groves of golden bliss to dwell....
But when he fell, with wingèd speed,
His champions, on a milk-white steed,
From the battle's hurricane,
Bore him to Joseph's tower'd fane,
In the fair isle of Avalon;
There, with chanted orison,
And the long blaze of tapers clear,
The stolèd fathers met the bier....
The faded tomb, with honour due,
'Tis thine, O Henry, to renew.

ANON

◀ *Glastonbury Thorn on Wearyall Hill*
◀ *Glastonbury Tor and drainage ditch*

Cattle below Glastonbury Tor
St Michael's Tower on
Glastonbury Tor

The continuity of tradition is not altogether broken, however, for the little street of Glastonbury has rather an old-time aspect, and one of the houses at least must have seen the last of the abbots ride abroad on his mule. The little inn is a capital bit of character, and as I waited for the 'bus under its low dark archway (in something of the mood, possibly, in which a train was once waited for at Coventry), and watched the barmaid flirting her way to and fro out of the heavy-browed kitchen and among the lounging young appraisers of colts and steers and barmaids, I might have imagined that the Merry England of the Tudors had not utterly passed away.

HENRY JAMES   1905

The most conspicuous object in the Vale of Avalon is a high, rounded hill, crowned with a lonely tower, rising beyond the ruins of Glastonbury. This hill is known as Glastonbury Tor, and the building is all that remains of the old pilgrimage chapel of St Michael.

In the early morning before the sun is strong, a man standing on this hill looks down, not upon the neat flat pasture lands of the Vale of Avalon, but upon Avalon, an island again, rising from a steaming sea of mist. In summer the mist rises from the fields as if it were the ghost of that sea which covered the valley in the age of legend. In the cold wind that runs before the dawn a man looks down upon this faint, moving veil, watches it writhe in spectral billows over the land, steaming upward in faint lines in the high places and so exposing the darker objects beneath which, in this hushed hour, seem almost like the bones of heroes, or the hulls of legendary barges sunk in some old poem.

HV MORTON   1927

◀   Glastonbury Tor Sunset

Pre-dawn at Glastonbury Tor   ▶

*"We should have to come here at midnight on Christmas Eve," said
John mysteriously. And I'll be sworn we saw some shadow of St.
Joseph and his companions that night on Wirral Hill, St. Joseph a
little, bent old man, and in his hand the staff that I have drawn
to-day, when twenty winters more have passed and scarcely touched
the leaning thorn. Legendary tree, having its roots in popular
tradition, grown too deep in Somersetshire soil for any Reformer to
destroy it, no earthquake of reason can overthrow it for one who as
a child has played in its blest shadow upon the holy ground of
Glastonbury, and still must haunt the place. In the cold sunlight of
an early spring, missing old company, I stood this morning a child
no longer, looking upon the thorn, which flowered at least a month
before the others of its kind, as the best that it might do by way of
witness to a sceptical age. The grass had grown over the ruins of
the great abbey, the branches of stone vaulting, the pillars like
forest trees, had long since been swept away like woods in a fire.*

FREDA DERRICK   1930

*1. Item. Certain persons to be sent to the Tower for the further
examination of the Abbot of Glaston.*

*2. Item. Councillors to give evidence against the Abbot of Glaston,
Richard Pollard, Lewis Forstell and Thomas Moyle.*

*3. Item. To see that the evidence is well sorted, and the indictment
well drawn against the said abbot and his complycys.*

*4. Item. The Abbot of Glaston to be tryed at Glaston and also executed
there with his complycys.*

THOMAS CROMWELL   1539

*T*HE GLASTONBURY *landscape is weird. Yet the essence of its weirdness is hard to catch. A green quilted acreage of reclaimed marsh stretches away and away toward the low Somersetshire ranges, toward the caves of Cheddar and the willows of Sedgemoor. In the centre, visible at vast distances and at queer angles, a skewed cone five hundred feet in height shatters the skyline. This is Glastonbury Tor. Two satellites attend it, Chalice Hill and Wearyall Hill. Between them and over them the houses of Glastonbury cluster and climb. Long walls enclose the battered remnants of a gigantic ecclesiastical building.*

GEOFFREY ASHE   1957

Pupil. What is this county peculiarly remarkable for?

Teacher. Not only for its being very extenſive and very populous, but for its profuſion of all the conveniencies of life.

P. I thank you ſir, I am fully convinc'd of the reaſon that you have given me for their ancient name ; but why, pray, are the preſent inhabitants of this place, called the natives of Somerſet?

T. Some hiſtorians are of opinion, that the county bears the title or appellation, on account of the air in thoſe parts being remarkably mild and gentle, and, as it were, a ſummer air; in which ſenſe the Britons, at this very day diſtinguiſhes it by the name of Gladerhaf, which bears exactly the ſame ſignification with our Engliſh term laſt mentioned.

THEOPHILUS BOTANISTA   1757

◀ *Field patterns from Walton Hill*

Field Gate Near Wedmore ▶

*T*aunton is a large town haveing houses of all sorts of buildings both brick and stone but mostly timber and plaister; its a very neate place and looks substantial as a place of good trade; you meete all sorts of country women wrapp'd up in the manteles called West Country rockets (rochets), a large mantle doubled together of a sort of serge, some are linsywolsey, and a deep fringe or fag at the lower end; these hang down some to their feete some only just below the wast, in the summer they are all in white garments of this sort, in the winter they are in red ones; I call them garments because they never go out without them and this is the universal fashion in Sommerset...

CELIA FIENNES   1685-1696

*T*aunton had long been famous not only for its own resources and for the spirit of its inhabitants, but also for the beautiful and highly cultivated country which spread around it, and gave rise to a gallant breed of yeomen. From time immemorial the town had been a rallying-point for the party of liberty, and for many years it had leaned to the side of Republicanism in politics and of Puritanism in religion. No place in the kingdom had fought more stoutly for the Parliament, and though it had been twice besieged by Goring, the burghers, headed by the brave Robert Blake, had fought so desperately, that the Royalists had been compelled each time to retire discomfited. On the second occasion the garrison had been reduced to dog's-flesh and horse-flesh, but no word of surrender had come either from them or their heroic commander, who was the same Blake under whom the old seaman Solomon Sprent had fought against the Dutch.

SIR ARTHUR CONAN DOYLE   1887

From Micah Clarke

◀ The castle Hotel, Taunton

Taunton Castle ▶

The steeple of the parish church of Bridgwater is said to be the loftiest in Somersetshire, and commands a wide view over the surrounding country. Monmouth, accompanied by some of his officers, went up to the top of the square tower from which the spire ascends, and observed through a telescope the position of the enemy. Beneath him lay a vast expanse, now rich with cornfields, but then, as its name imports, for the most part a dreary morass…When Monmouth looked upon Sedgemoor, it had been partially reclaimed by art, and was intersected by many deep and wide trenches which, in that country, are called rhines. In the midst of the moor rose, clustering round the towers of churches, a few villages, of whose names seem to indicate that they were once surrounded by waves. In one of these villages, called Westonzoyland, the royal cavalry lay; and Feversham had fixed his headquarters there.

T B MACAULAY   1848

From hence the winding Shore brings us to Bridgewater. This is an antient and very conſiderable Town and Port, it ſtands at the Mouth of the River Parrat, or Perot, which comes from the South, after having received the River Tone from the Weſt , which is made navigable up to Taunton, by a very fine new Channel, cut at the Expence of the People of Taunton, and which, by the Navigation of it, is infinitely advantagious to that Town, and well worth all their Expence, firſt by bringing up Coals, which are brought from Swanzy in Wales by Sea to Bridgewater, and thence by Barges up this River to Taunton; alſo for bringing all heavy Goods and Merchandizes from Briſtol, ſuch as Iron, Lead, Oyl, Wine, Hemp, Flax, Pitch, Tar, Grocery, and Dye Stuffs, and the like; their Tobacco they generally received from Barnſtaple by Land, which is about Sixteen Miles Weſt.

DANIEL DEFOE 1727

*I*n January last (towards the end of the moneth,) the sea at a flowing water meeting with Land-floudes, strove so violently together, that bearing downe all thinges yt were builded to withstand and hinder the force of them, the bankes were eaten through and a rupture made into Somerset-shire. No sooner was this furious invader entred, but he got up hie into the Land, and encountring with the river Severn, they both boild in such pride that many Miles, (to the quantity of XX. in length, and 4 or 5 at least in bredth) were in a short time swalowd up in this torrent. This Inundation began in the morning, & within few houres after, covered the face of ye earth thereabouts (that lay within the distance before named) to the deapth of XI. or XII. foot in some places, in others more. The daunger yt. this terrible tempest brought w' it wrought much fear in the harts of all that stood within the reach of it, but ye soden and strange cruelty of it, bred the greater terror and amazement. Men that were going to their labours were compelled (seeing so dreadfull an enemy approching) to flye backe to their houses, yet before they could enter, death stood at the dores ready to receive them. In a short tyme did whole villages stand like Islands (compassed rounde with Waters) and in a more short time were those Islands undiscoverable, and no where to be found. The tops of trees and houses onely appeared (especially there where the Countrey lay lowe) as if at the beginning of the world townes had been builte in the bottome of the Sea, and that people had plaide the husbandmen under the Waters.

ANON   1607

*O*ur road lay through Castle Carey and Somerton, which are
small towns lying in the midst of a most beautiful pastoral
country, well wooded and watered by many streams. The valleys
along the centre of which the road lies are rich and luxuriant,
sheltered from the winds by long rolling hills, which are themselves
highly cultivated. Here and there we passed the ivy-clad turret of
an old castle or the peaked gables of a rambling country house,
protruding from amongst the trees and marking the country seat of
some family of repute.

SIR ARTHUR CONAN DOYLE   1887

(From Micah Clarke)

◀ *Thatched Cottage at Puckington*

Cottage near Isle Abbotts ▶

*T*he drinking of cider in Somerset is not to be undertaken lightly by those who are unaware of its character. With the fizzy bottled stuff that is sold elsewhere it has little in common except the name. Cider drawn from the cask is truly a "wine of the country" in a land which has almost lost the meaning of the words. Taken in traditional style with the Cheddar cheese that came from the rich pastures of Sedgemoor and Avalon, it provided a simple meal of undoubted excellence.

DESMOND HAWKINS   1954

Stembridge Tower Windmill

Abbot's Fish House ▶

Yet all the time, just on the verge of this wickedly deceitful road, just beyond the tips of one's senses, just out of immediate reach, there is some of the most fascinating ground in all England ~ a countryside of subtle texture and numinous power, a landscape charged with distinctive beauties and mysteries that feed the imagination as few other English scenes can do. To define its special quality is not easy, though, albeit Sedgemoor and Avalon are words evocative enough in their way. But there is more to it than history, however poignant; more also than legend, however misty and alluring. The spirit of place is uncommonly strong here, and its essence is not easily captured.

DESMOND HAWKINS   1954

*T*here is no need to tell over again the story of the last battle fought upon English soil ~ how the attack of "King Monmouth's" levies was baulked by the Bussex Rhine ~ how Faversham allowed General Churchill to fight the battle, while he himself put on his best uniform and arranged his wig ~ how the Somersetshire clowns stood up to the Guards and the Tangier Brigade like heroes, and beat back the Blues pike in hand, fighting like old soldiers till the royal artillery shattered their ranks and all was over. It has been calculated that a loss of about one-sixth in killed and wounded is sufficient to unsteady average troops. Monmouth's raw levies endured heavier punishment than that before they broke. The story of the savage vengeance taken by James is perhaps the blackest in English history. Truly the memories which brood over the spire of Bridgwater and the tower of Weston Zoyland are grim and blood-stained.

*T*he engagement began between one and two of the clock in the morning. It continued near one hour and a half. There was killed upon the spot, of the King's soldiers, sixteen: five of them buried in the church: the rest in the churchyard; and they had all Christian burial. One hundred or more of the King's soldiers wounded, of which wounds many died: of which we have no certain account. There was killed of the rebels upon the spot, about 300: hanged with us, 22 - of which 4 were hanged in gemmaces (i.e. chains): about 500 prisoners brought into our church, of which there was 79 wounded, and 5 of them died of their wounds in our church.

RICHARD ALFORD   1665

◀ *West Moor*

Westonzoyland Church ▶

O ur road led us along the crest of the
Polden Hills, whence we had an
extensive and panoramic prospect of gloomy
Sedgemoor, famous as being the scene of the
last battle fought on English ground. It is a
dark-looking, melancholy region, cheerless in
spite of the warm sunshine, as though the
spirit of the past brooded over it, and as
though it still were in mourning for the
many brave men, friend and foe, who
slumber now side by side beneath its black
funereal soil.

JAMES JOHN HISSEY   1886

King's Sedgemoor Drain ◀

Pollarded trees on West Sedgemoor ▶

*T*herefore, said Arthur unto Sir Bedivere, take thou Excalibur, my good sword, and go with it to yonder water side, and when thou comest there I charge thee throw my sword in that water, and come again and tell me what thou there seest......

Then Sir Bedivere departed, and went to the sword, and lightly took it up, and went to the water side ; and there he bound the girdle about the hilts, and then he threw the sword as far into the water as he might ; and there came an arm and an hand above the water and met it, and caught it, and so shook it thrice and brandished, and then vanished away the hand with the sword in the water.

THOMAS MALORY   c1400

◀ *Pollarded trees near Burrowbridge Mump*
North Drain Nr. Wedmore ▶

Avalon's island, with avidity
Claiming the death of pagans,
More than all the world beside,
For the entombment of them all,
Honoured by chanting spheres of prophecy:
And for all time to come
Adornèd shall be
By them that praise the Highest.
Abbadarè, mighty in Saphat,
Noblest of pagans,
With countless thousands
There hath fallen on sleep.
Amid these Joseph in marble,
Of Arimathea by name,
Hath found perpetual sleep:
And he lies on a two-forked line
Next the south corner of an oratory
Fashioned of wattles
For the adoring of a mighty Virgin
By the aforesaid sphere-betokened
Dwellers in that place, thirteen in all.
For Joseph hath with him
In his sarcophagus
Two cruets, white and silver,
Filled with blood and sweat
Of the Prophet Jesus.
When his sarcophagus
Shall be found entire, intact,
In time to come, it shall be seen
And shall be open unto all the world;
Thenceforth nor water nor the dew of heaven
Shall fail the dwellers in that ancient isle,
For a long while before
The day of judgment in Josaphat
Open shall these things be
And declared to living men.

MAELGWN   5th Century

◀ *Butleigh Moor showing Polden Hill behind*

◀ *Godney with Glastonbury Tor in the distance*

*The cows of this district are intended
chiefly for the purposes of cheese-making.
The cheese is much admired, particularly that
made in the parishes of Meare and Cheddar.
It is for the most part purchased by jobbers,
and sent through the medium of Weyhill,
Giles's Hill, Reading and other fairs to the
London market, where it is sold under the
name of double Gloucester.*

JOHN BILLINGSLEY   1797

　　　Cattle grazing on The Levels ▶

*T*hen they might see and perceive afar of, as it were in the element, huge and mighty hilles of water, tombling one over another, in such sort, as if the greatest mountaines in the world had overwhelmed the lowe valeyes or marshy grounds. Sometimes it so dazled the eyes of many of the spectators, that they immagined it had bin some fogge or miste, comming with great swiftness towards them, and with such a smoke, as if mountaeyns were all on fire ; and, to the view of some, it seemed as if myllyons of thousands of arrowes had bin shot foorth all at one time, which came in such swiftness, as (it was verily thought) that the fowls of the ayre could scarse fly so fast; such was the threatning furyes thereof.

ANON   1607

A lbeit that these swelings up and overflowings of waters proceed from natural causes, yet are they the very diseases and monstrous byrthes of nature, sent into the world to terrifie it, and to put it in mind, yt. the great God, (who holdeth stormes in the prison of the Cloudes at his pleasure, and can enlarge them to breed disorder on the Earth when he growes angry) can as well now drowne all mankind as he did at the first: But yt. by these gentle warnings, he would rather have us come unto him, and flye from the points of more deadly Arrowes of vengeance, than utterly to perish.

ANON   1607

JOHN LELAND 1540-1542

◀ *Road near Glastonbury*

◀ *Bridge over drain*

Somerset Dawn
Burrowbridge Mump

Burrowbridge Mump

INDEX

The CAPITAL LETTER entries
are photographs

WRITERS

PHOTOGRAPHER'S NOTES

I have considered a book on Somerset for many years. Because of the uneven shape of the county I always considered it impossible. What does Exmoor have in common with Yeovil for instance? I just didn't see a visual harmony. Then last year in a frenzy of photography I captured enough material to begin a short book on Glastonbury. As I began to fill in the gaps this year, I realised that the Land of Avalon was providing more material than my earlier plans suggested. Everytime I set out with my camera I produced more good material.

My style often depends on using the first light of dawn to enhance the intensity of colours and textures and cast interesting shadows. I abhor the tendency of photographers in books like this to give paragraphs of technical detail. My most important pieces of equipment are a map, an alarm clock and a compass. Being there is the only advice I can give. Just to give some idea what good conditions will produce, the pictures on pages 29, 30, 34, 37, 38, 39, 41, 82, 88 and 89 were all taken on one day.

ATMOSPHERE also publish other books of Bob Croxford's
photographs in the same general format

All the books can be ordered at any good bookshop.
In case of difficulty phone 01326 240180 or
email books@atmosphere.co.uk

FROM CORNWALL WITH LOVE   *ISBN 09521850 0 8*
FROM DEVON WITH LOVE   *ISBN 09521850 1 6*
FROM BATH WITH LOVE   *ISBN 09521850 2 4*
FROM DORSET WITH LOVE   *ISBN 09521850 3 2*
FROM THE COTSWOLDS WITH LOVE   *ISBN 09521850 4 8*
HAMPSHIRE   *ISBN 09521850 5 9*

THE CORNISH COAST (115 x 165 size)   *ISBN 09521850 7 5*

ACKNOWLEDGEMENTS

Many thanks to Julie Simmonds and Karen Forster for their invaluable help

Thanks to Lynn and Michael Orchard for permission to photograph at Chalice Well.

The quotation from SOMERSET ANTHOLOGY by Roger Clark edited by Percy Lovell,
published by William Sessions Ltd is reproduced by kind permission of Percy Lovell
The quotation from KING ARTHUR'S AVALON by Geoffrey Ashe originally published by Collins is reproduced by kind permission of Geoffrey Ashe
The quotation from GOTHIC WANDERINGS IN SOMERSET by Freda Derrick is reproduced by kind permission of Philip H Smith
The quotation from OUR GAME by John le Carré published by Hodder & Stoughton is reproduced by kind permission of David Higham Associates
The quotation from STEINBECK: A LIFE IN LETTERS edited by Elaine Steinbeck and Robert Wallsten
published by Heinemann is reproduced by kind permission of Penguin UK
The quotations from SEDGEMOOR AND AVALON by Desmond Hawkins, published by Robert Hale
are reproduced by kind permission of David Higham Associates
The quotation from IN SEARCH OF ENGLAND by H V Morton is reproduced by permission of Methuen Publishing Ltd

Every effort has been made to contact all the copyright holders. Should the publishers have made any mistakes in attribution,
we will be pleased to make the necessary arrangements at the first opportunity.